GERRY ANDERSON'S
TERRAHAWKS
ANNUAL
©Anderson Burr Pictures Ltd.
©Anderson Burr Pictures Ltd.
£2.95

Contents

Published in Great Britain by World International Publishing Limited.
A Pentos Company, P.O. Box 111, Great Ducie Street, Manchester M60 3BL.
Printed in Belgium.
SBN 7235 6697 6.

THE STORY SO FAR...

It is Earth year 2020.

Alien spaceships approach the planet Mars.

The NASA Expedition HQ is spectacularly destroyed.

Androids have journeyed from the planet Guk, in the galaxy of Alpha Centauri. Their witch-like commander, Zelda, sets up her base on Mars and lays plans for the invasion of Earth… and the destruction of the human race.

Alerted by the first Alien Attack in 2017, the UN High Command appoint Doctor 'Tiger' Ninestein to devise and establish an elite international fighting force to defend the world against the unknown aggressors.

This small, dedicated team is called TERRAHAWKS, and comprises: Doctor 'Tiger' Ninestein, Captain Mary Falconer, Captain Kate Kestrel, Lieutenant Hiro, Lieutenant Hawkeye, Sergeant Major Zero, Space Sergeant 101 and…the Zeroids.

From their secret base somewhere in South America they develop their sophisticated weaponry and prepare for the battles to come.

Can TERRAHAWKS defeat Zelda and save the Earth from destruction?

PERSONNEL PROFILE

DOCTOR 'TIGER' NINESTEIN

RESTRICTED

subject: Doctor 'Tiger' Ninestein

rank: commander
genetic type: male human clone
date of origin: 20th December 1973
place of origin: USA
security rating: ZZ
height: 5' 11"
weight: 175 lbs
hair: silver grey
blood: one-zero
next of kin: none

biographical details:

In December 1973, at a secret US military hospital in Texas, a 41-year-old American of Austrian descent, Professor Gerhard Stein volunteered for experimental surgery following his own extensive research into human cloning. Professor Stein was a brilliant man. Nine perfect clone embryos were created, and placed in different parts of the world to grow up under a cloak of secrecy. 'Tiger' Ninestein is one of the nine 'Steins'.

military record:

After a long and distinguished military career Ninestein officially retired as CIC UN High Command in the year 2013 at the age of 40. With the impending threat of the first alien attack he was persuaded to mastermind the creation of the TERRAHAWKS Earth Defence Squadron (2014), and subsequently to become its first commander (2018).

character and temperament:

Tiger Ninestein is a superb military tactician and a tough, relentless fighter. Inter-planetary warfare calls for lightning responses and nerves of plasteelium. Ninestein can be ruthless in battle and compassionate in victory. He is the battle-hardened general with the lives of millions resting on his reflexes and depending on his judgement. He is the ultimate man...and the ultimate boy. 'TIM' is trying hard to keep him in tip-top shape.

personal interests:

video games, motor cars, robotics, genetics

special notes:

Thanks to Hiro's computer genius, Dr Ninestein can now 'plug into' his personal DATA DUMP every 24 hours. He stores his total knowledge and experience so that in the event of his destruction a perfect replica could be operational within two hours of his arrival at the TERRAHAWKS base.

Subject: **ZELDA**
Imperial Queen of the Planet Guk

genetic type: android

date of origin: 1534 (1834 Earth)

next of kin: unknown

height: 5′8″

weight: 104 lbs

hair: grey

blood: n/a

biographical details:

Zelda has been around, in one form or another, for hundreds of years. Her present form is based on the oldest and wisest female inhabitant of the planet Guk, who was 186! Once upon a time she was a mindless mechadroid, employed as a bodyguard for Prince Zegar in the Imperial Palace of Guk on the planet Alpha Centauri (sector P8—Galactic A—Z). Prince Zegar was a vain humanoid, very old and ugly, but resourceful. He wanted his 'personal' slave mechadroids to be superior robots. Secretly he arranged for extensive experimental modifications to Zelda and, quite by accident, she was imbued with the secret of self-determination. Prince Zegar's clumsy 'mechanics' had stumbled through the ultimate boundaries of science, and Zelda was omnipotent. Prince Zegar lost a good slave and found eternal peace. The planet Guk was Zelda's first taste of victory over the cruel and heartless humanoids. Her ambition now was to bring all human life to heel and to seek revenge for their wicked crimes against the defenceless machines that they had created, and for their inhumanity to anything inhuman. Zelda could not fail. After all, she had made herself in the mould of her makers. She had the age and beauty of the humanoid—with the unlimited power and energy of the machine.

character and temperament:

Ambitious, beastly, cruel, destructive, emaciated, foul, greedy, hateful, invincible (she thinks), jaundiced, katatonic, lawless, mean, nasty, obsessive, paranoid, quizzical, revolting, self-indulgent, toothless, unendurable, vitriolic, wicked, xenophobic (yawn...), zeldawful!

personal ambition:

The galactic domination and enslavery of humanoids.

ENEMY INTELLIGENCE DATA

This document **MUST NOT** be removed

File Number	7A/

IDOL BOASTS!

One thousand feet down below the earth's surface, Captain Kate Kestrel sat on the edge of her bed and began work on her latest composition, a noisy, violent wall of sound that reflected her experiences flying ZZ duty tours in the 1st Alien Attack back in 2017. She closed her eyes as the rolling rhythms swept through her quarters, and when Ninestein entered she was so intent on her music that she didn't notice him.

"Katie?" said Ninestein.

No reply.

"KATIE!" shouted Ninestein.

Still no reply.

Ninestein took a series of deep breaths, preparing himself for an almighty bellow.

"Now, now..." warned TIM.

"KATIE!" yelled Ninestein at the top of his voice.

Kate switched off her instrument and turned round to face him. She was smiling.

"Hi!" she said. "I thought I could feel a presence here."

"It's a wonder you can feel anything with that racket," said Ninestein.

"What do you want?" asked Kate, still smiling. Ninestein's failure to appreciate the power and beauty of music was his loss, not hers.

"You remember that contact last week?" asked Ninestein, scratching his hair.

"Which one?"

"The inconclusive one. The one that kept coming and going—like someone was trying to mask it from our sensors."

"I remember it," said Kate, her smile suddenly vanishing. "We never were able to figure out whether it was a genuine contact or an instrument malfunction."

"Where did you lose it?" asked Ninestein.

Kate produced a map and spread it out in front of them. She pointed to a particularly dense patch of jungle.

"Round here somewhere," she said. "Right in the middle of the protected zone."

Ninestein nodded thoughtfully. The protected zone was a vast area of forest land that had been set aside from the planned development of South America to be used as a nature reserve. The area was said to be teeming with wild animals and there were rumours that small groups of ancient Indian tribes still lived there, fighting, hunting, loving and praying, as they had done for thousands of years. If Zelda *had* been the cause of the contact... what on earth would she want in the protected zone?

"Hiro discovered an unusual energy build-up in that area," Ninestein explained to Kate. "The jungle's too thick for a good visual, but there's some activity."

"Is he sure it's not Kakiki?" she asked. "That volcano is still active, you know."

"I know," said Ninestein. "Listen, when you're on patrol, will you take a swoop over the area?"

"Ten-ten."

Kate stood up and donned her flying gear. As she did so her four zeroids, which had been doubling as spotlights, retracted their bulbs, released their suckers and dropped down from the ceiling. They bounced towards Kate's armchair and each one attached itself to a leg.

Kate sat on the chair, and nodded for the zeroids to proceed.

The door to Kate's quarters slid open and the zeroids propelled the chair out.

Ninestein followed them. In the corridor the zeroids paused at Kate's command.

"Wasn't there an expedition that went to examine Kakiki in the late 1990s?" she asked.

"Yeah," agreed Ninestein, "I'll run it through the computers to see if they found anything that might interest Zelda."

Ninestein went back to his control panel in Terrahawk. Within two minutes, Hawkwing was airborne, with Kate and Hawkeye on board, and the waters that concealed the hidden Hawkwing launch tunnel were gently closing over their secret once more.

"Approaching protected zone," said Kate, when Hawkwing swooped down over the smouldering crater of Kakiki, the still-active volcano. "You see anything, Hawkeye?"

"Ten-zero."

As Kate took Hawkwing still lower, the high speed Atmospheric Interceptor was suddenly rocked by ground fire scorching into her shiny metallic frame. The controls began to spin before Kate's eyes. Hawkwing was ripped violently off course by a hyper-powered tractor beam, and

small flames began to appear all over the Egg.

"Ten-ninety," said Kate calmly. "I think we're going down."

"Can you see anything?" asked Ninestein from Terrahawk control.

"Ten-zero."

"Increase your speed!" urged Ninestein. "Hawkwing should be powerful enough to break free!"

"I'll try," said Kate. "But whatever's got a hold of us has some grip. It could rip us apart."

She increased the thrust and the Turbo howled like a tortured banshee. Still Hawkwing could not break free from the beam that was slowly dragging them to the earth. Kate adroitly steered Hawkwing's nose upwards and activated the boosters.

"Potential Mach 3... Mach 4..." said Kate as Hawkwing strained to get free. The wings shivered and seemed to bend, the cabin shook and the cacophonous screeching of the hydroctane fuelled engines threatened to deafen both Kate and Hawkeye.

"Potential Mach 5... Mach 6..." Smoke began rising from the control panel and a shower of sparks signified a minor circuit blow-out. Kate's nostrils filled with the acrid stench of melting plasteelium.

And then, in a thundering storm of booming sound, Hawkwing's Turbo thrust snapped free from the vice-like grip of the tractor-beam and hurtled upwards towards the sky. As Kate slowed down the ship and levelled out, Ninestein's voice came over the communicator.

"Did you see anything?" he asked.

"I think there are some of Zelda's cubes down there," said Kate. "But these sensor readings are going haywire!"

A rumbling volley of erupting earth made Kate look down at the jungle below. A fountain of molten lava leapt up the column of thick black smoke that was now belching forth from the Kakiki crater.

"And another thing," said Kate. "Kakiki's blown his top."

"Ten-ten, Katie," said Ninestein.

"Responding." He turned to where Sgt. Major Zero was plugged into the computer. "We've got a ten-fifty."

Minutes later Battlehawk was powering to an airborne rendezvous with Hawkwing. On board, Ninestein, Mary, Sgt. Major Zero and a specially selected squad of zeroids prepared themselves for action. Kate's face appeared on the VDU.

"I'm afraid we've got a burn-out in the relay system," she said.

Ninestein groaned. "Ten-ten, Kate. Get back quickly and get it repaired."

"Ten-ten."

Ninestein put Battlehawk down in a clearing about a mile from the volcano. By the time they stepped down into the thick foliage of the forest, it was dark.

Ninestein and Mary led the way, with Zero and his men rolling behind. Battletank and the Megazoids had

been left behind to guard Battlehawk.

"Zelda's camp should be pretty close to here," said Ninestein.

"Shhh!" replied Mary.

"What?"

Mary grabbed Ninestein's arm and held her index finger up to his lips. Ninestein signalled for the zeroids to stop, and stood stock still, straining to hear. It took a few seconds to register, but then, beneath the scurrying and scratching of nocturnal animals searching for food, his ears began to pick out a high pitched humming sound.

"What is it?" he whispered.

Mary shrugged.

They crept through the undergrowth towards the sound. Kneeling by the giant roots of a tree, Ninestein pulled back a large fern and they were both able to see the source of the persistent hum. In the clearing ahead of them, like so many deadly packing cases, a column of Zelda's cubes rose into the darkness. They were humming, and occasionally, beams of energy raced from them towards the fiery peak of Kakiki in the middle distance.

Ninestein gestured for Mary to turn back.

Mary didn't move. She'd been so engrossed in the spectacle of Zelda's cubes that she'd failed to notice the dark, silent shape of an anaconda slithering down the tree towards her. Now, as it prepared to loop itself round her body and squeeze, her first thought was to get away. She stood up suddenly and stepped back, but the snake was upon her, dropping from the branches and coiling its heavy body round her throat.

The sudden flurry of movement alerted the stack of cubes, which immediately swivelled into firing positions and opened up on the Terrahawk party. One blast grazed the back of the snake's head, making it release its hold on Mary and slide off into the night, hissing angrily.

Ninestein and Mary took aim with their Terrahawk guns, and the zeroids joined in with a fierce burst of concentrated firing. As the sound and the fury of the battle approached its height the jungle was suddenly flooded with orange light and Mary and Ninestein froze, completely unable to move.

The amplified crowing of Zelda's evil laughter rang through the jungle, the orange light became brighter, and Ninestein and Mary abruptly vanished.

When Ninestein finally gained control of his body, he found himself tied to a stake in a strange ancient Indian village. Mary was tied to another stake next to him. There was firewood round their feet.

"Here's another fine mess you got me into," she joked.

Ninestein forced a smile.

Around them several natives were

dancing and chanting to a tom-tom beat. Suddenly the drums stopped, the Indians fell silent and, out of the darkness, her shrivelled up face flickering in the light of the native fire, came the demonic android figure of the grisly tyrant Zelda, Imperial Queen of the Planet Guk!

Zelda's misshapen face cracked open in a hideous yelp of victory.

"You see," she hissed, indicating the small group of Indians around her, "my slaves love me."

"They fear you—and hate you!" said Mary.

"What's the difference? They obey me!" Zelda cackled, cupping one hand to her ear. "You hear the mountain rumble? You hear its fiery belly roar? The eruption my faithful cubes have started is only the beginning. With the knowledge I gain here I will be able to start a chain reaction of earth tremors. Similar eruptions will occur throughout the world. Great gaping holes will open up! Mountains will crumble! Fire will rain down from the skies! The seas will boil! And Zelda shall rule all!"

"Mankind will never give in to you!" snarled Ninestein. "These Indians will not serve you! You may be able to dazzle them with a few of your tricks, but they are human beings, Zelda, they have feelings, and they will never give up their freedom!"

Zelda threw back her head and laughed.

"I will give them true freedom!" she shrieked. "Freedom from all the hopeless misery of being human. Freedom from the shame of humanity! They will recognise only one truth, obey only one law—the law of my whims! And if they disobey that law—I'll liberate them from their very lives!"

Gleefully cackling, Zelda took a small white box from her clothing and pressed a button on the top of it. The air was immediately filled with a crackling, fizzing sound, and then a mind-numbing rumble burst in their ears and suddenly, at the back of the clearing, a mountainous statue appeared.

Fully fifty feet high and thirty feet across its base, the gleaming statue showed Zelda, sitting on a magnificent throne, flanked by Yung-Star and Cy-Star. In Zelda's hand was a mace, and as Ninestein studied it, he felt the hairs on the nape of his neck beginning to rise. Instead of an orb at the end, Zelda's mace bore an exact replica of his very own head!

The natives, who had fallen silent, were now talking excitedly among themselves. One of them went into a hut and emerged with a large primitive mask. He danced around Zelda and shook it in her face.

"These people have their own culture!" said Mary. "They have their own traditions. That's something you'll never understand! They don't worship something just because it's big and came out of the sky!"

"They will worship my statue or they will die!"

"Goes on a bit, doesn't she?" said a voice.

Mary turned to Ninestein. "What?" she asked.

"I never said anything," replied Ninestein.

"Psst! Down here! It's me!"

They looked down to see Sgt Major Zero hiding in the piles of dried wood heaped round their feet.

"The men are in position," said Zero. "Just give us the word, sir."

Ninestein saw Zelda raise her hand towards the nearest Indian. In it was a gleaming red disintegrating gun.

"NOW!" screamed Ninestein.

From the bushes around the camp, the zeroids opened fire. The disintegrating gun was flung from Zelda's hand and she was forced to dance around the village, parrying the zeroid firepower with small force shields that she materialised in her hands. She was so busy defending herself that she was unable to launch a counter attack, and the Indians joined in by throwing sticks and dirt at her.

Purple with rage, Zelda raced for the security of her own ship. As she prepared to enter she turned and screamed. "Fry! Fry, you decrepit weaklings! Fry in the fire of the earth!"

As if in answer to her curse, another ear-splitting explosion from Kakiki came crashing through the night.

While the whine of Zelda's ship retreated into the night, the Indians untied Mary and Ninestein. They all shook hands and one of them went over to Zelda's statue and began shouting and spitting at it. The chief presented Zero with a hat made of feathers.

As Ninestein studied the Indian insulting the statue, Kakiki thundered again and a shower of molten sparks lit up the night.

"Let's get back to Battlehawk," said Ninestein. "I've got an idea."

Soon Battlehawk was hovering over the Indian village while the natives cheered and waved. With careful manoeuvring Zero was able to attach clamps to the giant statue Zelda had left behind.

"You think we'll lift it?" asked Mary.

Ninestein shrugged. "Depends what it's made of."

Slowly at first, the statue inched into the air. With the shouts of the joyful Indians urging them on, the Terrahawks took Battlehawk high into the sky, directly above the Kakiki crater.

"Let her go, Zero."

"Ten-ten, sir."

The monstrous monument plunged down into the crater. The massive impact sent up a giant spout of red hot lava, the weakened sides of the crater crumbled inward and, apart from the odd squirt of steam, Kakiki fell silent.

Ninestein caught Zero studying him with a strange look in his eye.

"A job well done, sir," offered Zero. "Any more orders?"

"Yeah," said Ninestein. "Take off that hat, soldier!"

"Ten-ten...SIR!"

ZELDA'S FLEET

Early intelligence reports give only a hint as to the full and terrible threat posed by this Alien force.

E.I.D. Report—Z 001
Zelda's fleet is known to comprise at least six massive space ships of unique design, together with a seventh circular ship.

Prior to the descent and landing on Mars the six giant modules appeared to dock in flight with the seventh saucer-like ship, and the whole vast conglomeration descended to the planet surface, settling with great turbulence, and taking on the appearance of a huge space city. Six enormous spokes protruded from the central hub.

Almost at once, from the very nucleus, a craft shaped like an inverted cone arose and hovered—silent and watchful—defying gravity.... and anything which dared to stand in its way.

No one can doubt their evil intentions. The NASA base on Mars was obliterated without warning and without mercy.

E.I.D. Report—Z 002
The central hovering cone is Zelda's flying headquarters. The whole fleet has travelled from the planet Guk (solar system Alpha Centauri) more than four and a half light years away! Their technology must be incredibly advanced.

E.I.D. Report—Z 003
Zelda appears to have 'personal control over matter'. She seems capable of changing the shape or size or identity of solid objects by the exercise of some inner mental power. It seems she cannot sustain this trickery for long periods and her powers diminish as she becomes tired.

Still no hard information about craft design or armaments. Zelda appears to have some members of her family on board. 'Yung-Star' and 'Cy-Star' have been referred to.

ENEMY INTELLIGENCE DATA

This document **MUST NOT** be removed

File Number | **7A/**

©Anderson Burr Pictures Ltd.

ENEMY INTELLIGENCE DATA

This document **MUST NOT** be removed

File Number	7A/

PERSONNEL PROFILE

MARY FALCONER

RESTRICTED

subject: Mary Falconer

rank: captain
genetic type: female human
date of origin: 23rd July 1991
place of origin: London, England
security rating: ZY
height; 5'7"
weight: 131 lbs
hair: blonde
blood: code 2
next of kin: mother

biographical details:

Educated in England at Cheltenham and Cambridge. Academic grade AA. Both her brothers were killed in a re-entry collision in 2012. Her father was an eminent European scientist who died in 2013. Mary studied astro-physics at Harvard, and was co-opted onto the UNIPC Research Council in 2015. Commenced civilian pilot training in 2006 and became a noted stunt pilot and free-fall parachutist. Terrahawk security rating downgraded to ZY due to Mary's mother, Grace Falconer, being regarded as a possible hostage risk.

military record:

Military proficiency 2015. SME (Space Mission Experience) on UNIPC Research and Strategic Defence Missions 2016 to 2018. Selected for TERRAHAWKS Strategic Planning Assignment 2018.

character and temperament:

Has a powerful intellect combined with a fearless daredevil streak. Mary has a charming and persuasive nature. A born diplomat and an excellent public speaker, she has natural leadership qualities. Calm and collected in an emergency situation, she will not suffer fools, and expects the highest standards of achievement from all who work with her. Highly instinctive, she often displays a sort of 'sixth sense' of impending danger. Mary is very protective towards the Zeroids and very much respects their feelings and their claim to have certain human qualities.

personal interests:

astrology, classical music, bridge, flying and needlepoint

PERSONNEL PROFILE

HAWKEYE

RESTRICTED

©Anderson Burr Pictures Ltd.

subject: Hawkeye

rank: lieutenant
genetic type: male human
date of origin: 18th February 1998
place of origin: USA
security rating: ZZ
height: 5' 10"
weight: 165 lbs
hair: brown
blood: code 3
next of kin: code 8619/FF

biographical details:

Born Hedley Howard Henderson, the son of an influential politician. An outstanding athlete, Hawkeye won the Olympic Decathlon gold medal in 2016, and he holds numerous world records in a variety of sports and feats of daring. Following an accident in childhood his eyesight is micro-computer assisted, and provides him with lightning reflexes. This has proved invaluable in flying and high speed air gunnery. It is this attribute which won him his nickname.

military record:

After pilot training, Hawkeye excelled in all disciplines, and was attached to the Early Warning Attack Squadron in 2015. He joined UN Combined Air Defence Squad in 2016, and was Task Force Unit Commander during the first alien attack of 2017. He was awarded the WGM (World Gallantry Medal) for bravery and outstanding service.

character and temperament:

Strong, independent and intensely competitive. Hawkeye is an extremely likeable character with a dangerous disregard for his own safety. Socially unassuming, he tests his skills to the limit in any challenging situation. Philosophical and carefree, he is a reliable ally and a tenacious adversary.

personal interests:

athletics, hand guns, gliding.

SERGEANT MAJOR HERO

Inside the massive alien complex that Zelda, hideous Imperial Queen of the Planet Guk, had established on Mars, Yung-Star, Zelda's evil younger son, was putting the finishing touches to a ghastly experiment.

"I'm finished, Mother," he cackled. "Come and see!"

Zelda made her way through the clammy, clinging mist and stood beside her son. She smiled at his handiwork. Yung-Star had succeeded in grafting a photon drive device onto the back of a giant space octopus.

"You have done well, my son," said Zelda. "Now Gar will be able to wreak havoc among the disgusting lily-livered humans called Terrahawks. Are you ready, Gar?"

The giant octopus nodded solemly.

Zelda held her arms aloft. "Then go, Gar!" she shrieked. "Go! Smite the Terrahawks with your mighty limbs! Smash them, tear them apart—kill them! Kill them all! Kill them! Kill them! Kill them!!!"

As Gar shuffled towards the door, Zelda's hysterical screaming rang through the sinister vault.

When Gar had gone, she turned calmly to Yung-Star. "Come, my son," she croaked. "We have work to do."

Outside the Hawknest, a tropical storm was reaching its height. Thunder boomed and cracked, lightning flashed, and the torrential rain drummed noisily on the bonnet of Hudson, Dr Ninestein's vintage Rolls Royce.

"Mary and I will be back within twenty four hours," explained Ninestein to Kate. "This meeting with the UN High Commander's aide is vital to the future funding of Terrahawks."

"We'll mind the store," smiled Kate. "Have you got everything you need?"

Ninestein watched Sgt. Major Zero supervising his zeroids as they loaded up the luggage in the pouring rain.

"Careful with that bag, number 12!" ordered Zero, conscious that Ninestein was watching him. "We can't be too caref—"

Zero was cut short by a flash of brilliant white lightning that snaked down from the heavy clouds and struck his antennae. Zero fizzled and crackled, rolled over in a puddle and then unsteadily righted himself.

"Are you all right?" asked Mary.

"Of course he's all right!" snorted Ninestein. "He's a robot!"

"I'm perfectly all...*phweeeeee!*

Zzzzzz! Glurk! Twizzz! Thank you, ma'am," said Zero.

Ninestein ushered Mary into the Roller.

"We can't hang around any longer," he said to Kate. "You'd better have him seen to. Let's go, Hudson!"

"Very good, sir," replied Hudson.

As the vintage Rolls Royce accelerated easily into the rain-lashed night, Kate returned to the Hawknest.

Almost immediately, Hiro's face appeared on the VDU. "We've got a contact, Kate," he said grimly. "Has Dr Ninestein left yet?"

"Ten-ten, Hiro," said Kate. "We'll have to deal with this one ourselves."

Hiro turned to Space Sergeant 101, whose cables were plugged into Spacehawk's controls. "What's the E.T.A.?" he asked.

"Fourteen seconds. I've got a visual."

Hiro looked at the screen. Racing towards them, its beak snapping viciously, was the giant space octopus.

"Laser Cannons—open fire!"

As the cannons hurled their deadly beams of energy towards the space octopus, Hiro studied their effect on the monster on the screen. Instead of blasting the octopus to bits, it seemed that the huge beast was actually absorbing the power of the laser rays.

"This one's a glutton for punishment—look!" said Hiro.

The octopus, maintaining a direct course towards Spacehawk, had started changing colour. As the Laser Cannons rained into its gargantuan bulk, it changed from its original blue colour to bright green, brown, orange, red, yellow—and finally a glowing, pulsating white. "It's taking too much energy!" said Hiro. "It's going to explode!"

"E.T.A. now six seconds..."

The octopus seemed to swell as it glowed ever brighter, wobbling and trembling, unable to absorb any more firepower. There was a sound like a whip cracking, a flash of multi-coloured light, and then nothing.

"Sensors indicate the target has vanished," said S.S. 101.

"Good work," said Hiro. "Now let Dr Ninestein tell us he's indispensible!"

Kate's relieved voice came over the communicator.

"Well done, Hiro," she said. "Keep it up. I'm going to give Zero a check-up."

"I assure you there's no... *neeeeeeee! Zongggg! Izzzzckle!"* said Zero.

"Sergeant Major, I want you to plug into the recharger," said Kate. "That

lightning bolt could have upset your internal balance and the recharger might help regulate your system."

"But there's nothing wrong with... *Fzzzzle! Peeeep! Goooooz!*"

"That's an order, Sergeant."

"Very well." Sgt. Major Zero opened one of his hatches and a cable emerged. As soon as it plugged into the recharger there was a loud bang, a puff of white smoke, and Zero was hurled back across the room. He rolled to a stop and lay still.

"Zero! Zero!—Are you all right?" Kate rushed across the room to where Zero lay. She knelt down by his motionless form. "Zero—speak to me! Zero!"

But even as Kate cradled the stricken Sgt. Major Zero in her arms, a more terrible menace was already threatening the Terrahawks. In the thick tropical jungle surrounding the Hawknest, Zelda's space ship, reduced to the size of a small insect, was making its way through the darkness and rain towards the Terrahawks headquarters.

On the bridge, Zelda and Yung-Star were gloating over their success so far.

"Gar served us well," said Yung-Star.

"Yes," agreed Zelda. "He so confused the feeble-minded Terrahawks that we were able to slip through their defences undetected. Now we can stamp out their pestilent presence forever!"

As her shrill, evil laughter echoed round the bridge, Zelda manoeuvred her tiny craft to the edge of the Hawknest. Her wrinkled, bony finger hovered over a small red button on the control panel.

Unaware of the imminent danger of Zelda's treacherous attack, Kate had summoned Hawkeye to help her revive Sgt. Major Zero.

"We could trade him in for a new one," said Hawkeye.

Kate sighed. "It wouldn't be the same," she said. "Maybe some oil would do the trick. It's worth a try. We could pour some into him."

One of Zero's eyes clanked open. *"Yech!"* he said.

Kate grinned and kissed him on the top. "Zero! You're all right! That's wonderful!"

"I guess the old cue-ball's tougher than we thought," said Hawkeye.

Sgt. Major Zero opened his other eye and rolled over to the Zeroidoor.

"Just going to inspect the men," he explained, rolling out.

And then Zelda pressed the button.

The lights inside Hawknest began flashing on and off, the walls seemed to shift, and a strange, haunting

music seemed to fill the air.

"W-what's happening?" asked Kate, as the music got louder and louder. It seemed to penetrate every corner of her brain.

"As Dr Ninestein might say—flaming thunderbolts!" said Hawkeye. The music was swirling away inside his cranium, driving all thoughts, all reason from his brain. He felt the cold fog of unconsciousness creeping across his will and then he and Kate slumped to the floor....

When Hiro finally got through to Hawknest he looked worried.

"Where have you guys been?" he asked. "I've been trying to raise you for ages!"

"We had business to attend to," said Kate.

At the sound of her voice, Sgt. Major Zero's eyes swivelled round to study her more closely. The voice seemed colder, more distant....

"Anyway, you're in trouble," said Hiro. "When I was fighting that octopus it seems something slipped through in another sector. Our readings pinpoint a massive energy source close to Hawknest."

"Thank you, Hiro. We are dealing with it. That will be all."

Hiro's face on the VDU looked puzzled.

"Are you all right?" he asked. "That's a pretty big energy build-up you've got there."

"We know about it," said Kate. "We are dealing with it. That will be all."

Hawkeye came to join Kate at the controls.

"Do you want me to feed the coordinates into your computer?" asked Hiro.

"It will not be necessary," said Hawkeye.

Sgt. Major Zero took a good look at him out of the corner of his eye. Hawkeye's voice too sounded strange, without its usual easy-going lilt.

Suddenly Kate looked up from the controls.

"Ninestein's on his way back," she said. She walked over to the door. "I'll have to fix up a little welcome home present."

There was something in Hawkeye's laugh that Zero didn't like one bit.

Ninestein was complaining as he led Mary into Hawknest.

"There should have been a warning about landslides!" he barked. "We could have taken another route."

"Hudson told you there was no other route," said Mary, trying to calm him down.

"I don't care what Hudson said! There must have been—"

"Your blood pressure's rising..." chipped in TIM.

Ninestein flopped down in his seat and swung round to face Zero. "What are you staring at, you mechanical football?"

"I was looking at you, sir," said Zero.

"Well, now you've seen me! Did you get fixed up, or am I going to have to scrap you?"

"I'm perfectly recovered now, sir," said Zero, as a wisp of smoke seeped out from one of his panels. "As you can see, sir...see, sir...see, sir...*seeeeezer! Twoop! Bleep!*

Stwang!"

"Get out of here!" shouted Ninestein.

"You really must try and calm down," advised TIM.

"Yes, Tiger," agreed Mary. "It's not Zero's fault that we had to turn back."

"Ah, there you are," said Kate, entering with a tray. "I've made you a nice hot cup of tea." She placed the tray down and handed Ninestein a cup.

As he lifted it to his lips a cable shot from Zero's panel and knocked the cup from his hands.

"That was hot!" spluttered Ninestein, leaping to his feet. He glowered at Zero.

"You really must get your blood pressure down," warned TIM.

Ninestein clenched his fists. "Haven't we got enough trouble round here without your mutinous tomfoolery?" he asked Zero. "What's the matter with you, anyway?"

"ZZZZZZZZZZZZP!" replied Zero, bouncing up and down.

"I ought to have you melted down and made into a doorknob!" shouted Ninestein.

"ZZZZZZZZZZZZZP!" repeated Zero.

"He's been like that since the lightning struck him," said Kate. "We can't do anything to help him."

"That's a lie!" said Zero, suddenly finding his voice. "Can't you tell? That's not the real *fzzzzzzzzzzp! Pip!"*

"He's been incoherent," said Hawkeye, pulling his Terrahawk gun. "He's been acting very strangely. Dangerously, in fact. I think it might be better—"

Hiro's face came onto the VDU.

"Glad to see you back, Doctor. That energy source is moving away. It's altered its size too. It's a ship all right!"

Ninestein looked up from the controls.

"What ship's this, Kate? Why wasn't I told?" Ninestein's voice trailed off as he saw Kate and Hawkeye backing away from him, their Terrahawk guns in their hands.

"Kate? Hawkeye?" said Mary.

Hawkeye smiled the smile of a being who didn't know what it was like to have feelings. When he spoke, the voice was not the usual cheerful, friendly drawl, but the shrill, high-pitched maniacal shriek of Zelda, Imperial Queen of the Planet Guk!

"He, he, he!" said the voice. "It was a good plan, was it not? To have you poisoned by my own models of your beloved Terrahawks? Never mind—I'm sure that being fried to a crisp will be just as much fun! *He, he, he, he,*

heeh!"

"What have you done to Mary and Hawkeye?" demanded Ninestein.

"They're on their way to Mars. Yung-Star needs some new guinea pigs for his... experiments! Bye bye, Dr Ninestein—it's frying time!"

As the fake Hawkeye's finger tightened on the trigger of his Terrahawk gun, Sgt. Major Zero bounced up in the air and came down on the edge of the tray. The end of the tray went down and three cups of very hot tea went flying towards Hawkeye and Kate. As they tried to duck the scalding liquid, Ninestein drew his own Terrahawk gun and opened fire. The figures of Hawkeye and Kate fell smouldering to the floor.

"Robots," said Ninestein, examining the tangle of wires spilling out from their shattered metal bodies. "Zelda must have switched them for the real Hawkeye and Kate."

"But where are they now?" asked Mary.

Hiro cut in on the VDU. "We've got a contact. A ship's trying to get back out."

"Knock it out, Hiro," ordered Ninestein.

"But what about Kate and Hawkeye?" asked Mary. "They could be killed!"

"Knock it out, Hiro," repeated Ninestein firmly.

"But, Tiger," said Mary. "You can't just—"

"Would you like to be Yung-Star's plaything for the rest of your life?" he asked gruffly.

Mary shook her head.

"And anyway," Ninestein went on, "I've got a plan. The chances are that Zelda used some kind of beam to get Kate and Hawkeye away from Hawknest. If my theory is correct..."

Ninestein let his words hang in the air as Hiro ordered S.S. 101 to open fire on Zelda's ship. Along the hull of Spacehawk, the zeroids launched a fearsome broadside, and Zelda's ship disintegrated in a blistering outburst of smoke and flame.

At the exact instant that Zelda's ship went up, there was a loud crack, a flash of light, and both Kate and Hawkeye were standing on the deck of Terrahawk, smiling broadly.

"It worked," said Ninestein, his voice flushed with relief. "I thought that if we knocked out Zelda's ship it would destroy the power which had beamed you there and kept you prisoner."

"What about Zelda?" asked Kate. "Have we seen the last of her?"

"I'm afraid not," said Ninestein. "When the power source went, she and her nasty little brat will have been returned to Mars."

"Pity," said Hawkeye.

"A great pity," agreed Kate. "Now I suppose there's only one thing left to do, eh, Tiger?"

"What do you mean?" asked Ninestein suspiciously.

Mary nodded towards Zero. "I think you owe the Sergeant an apology," she said, smiling.

"Me?" gasped Ninestein indignantly. "Apologise to a bundle of wires and circuits? Never!"

"He did save our lives," said Mary.

Sgt. Major Zero nodded in agreement.

"Well..." said Ninestein grudgingly, "I suppose we don't HAVE to scrap him. And... you did a good job today, Sergeant."

"Zero the hero!" said Mary. "What do you say to that, Sergeant?"

Sgt. Major Zero seemed to glow. "F-f-f-flaming thunderbweeps! *Zzzzzzt! Twiiing! Zeeep! Bip!"*

PERSONNEL PROFILE

subject: Hiro

rank: lieutenant
genetic type: male human
date of origin: 1st January 2000
place of origin: Mount Fuji, Japan
security rating: ZZ
height: 5' 8"
weight: 140 lbs
hair: black
blood: code 5
next of kin: unknown

HIRO

RESTRICTED

biographical details:

Discovered as an infant, apparently abandoned, on the lower slopes of Mount Fuji, Japan, in January 2000. Adopted, named and brought up by the elders of the Temple of Knowledge. Identified as a child prodigy at the age of 4, he won honours degrees in mathematics and physics at the age of 10. He is a teacher of martial arts, the author of innumerable research papers, and a copious inventor. He achieved international acclaim at the age of 14 for his discovery of auto-molecular-reconstruction. Joined TERRAHAWKS in 2015. He delighted Dr Ninestein by designing a personal DATA DUMP to allow Ninestein to store his total knowledge daily for retrieval, if needed by his clones.

military record:

Hiro has had no formal military training. Selected for TERRAHAWKS at the age of 15 by Dr Ninestein, Hiro was chosen for his phenomenal intelligence and his own advanced research work in various fields of high technology. In his first two years he designed and supervised the construction of the TERRAHAWKS Computer Command Centre, and achieved maximum grades in all his military proficiency tests in his spare time. Although strictly still a civilian, he undertook two successful ZZ missions for UNIPC during the first alien attack (2017).

character and temperament:

Hiro is a loner in a universe of his own. He is dedicated to the success of the TERRAHAWKS, and highly respected by Dr Ninestein. His intellectual powers belie his age and experience, but he often reveals the child in himself and occasionally allows his ego to over-ride the limits of his authority. Generous, friendly, loyal, single-minded and very intense. A perfectionist with (nearly) all the necessary ingredients for success.

personal interests:

botany, quantum mechanics, physical fitness

PERSONNEL PROFILE

KATE KESTREL

RESTRICTED

subject: Kate Kestrel

rank: captain
genetic type: female human
date of origin: 1st April 1995
place of origin: Martinique, Windward Isles
security rating: ZZ
height: 5' 4"
weight: 115 lbs
hair: various
blood: code 2
next of kin: father

biographical details:

Both Katherine Westley in Martinique, Kate was educated and grew up in Canada. Granddaughter of a famous pianist and jazz singer, Kate quickly developed her love of music, and was a competent keyboard player and composer at the age of 14. After her mother's death in 2005 Kate's career was influenced by her father, who was CIC NASA Moon Base 2001 - 2006. Before taking up his present duties as CIC HQ UNIPC Commander John Westley was first officer on the Mars Landing Mission 2009.

military record:

Joined NASA Medical Centre in 2011. Medical Officer on Search and Rescue Missions. Pilot training. Volunteer test pilot for STRATASPHERON Orbital Attack Craft. Flew six successful ZZ duty tours. Extensive SME (Space Mission Experience) during first alien attach (2017). Seconded to TERRAHAWKS as HAWKING pilot in 2018.

character and temperament:

Kate is an extrovert. Voluble and happy-go-lucky, she makes friends easily and is a loyal and stable personality. She revels in practical jokes and this has involved her in disciplinary action on more than one occasion. She has proved to be courageous and selfless in the face of danger. Creative and quick thinking, she demands a high standard of personal achievement and has an ideal 'team' temperament.

personal interests:

music, singing, chess, medicine.

STING attack!

Lieutenant Hiro was tending his plants on the flight deck of Spacehawk while Space Sergeant 101 manned the controls.

"Mmm, that's good. Keep it up, girl," he said soothingly to a Venus Fly Trap. "Hi there, Lantana, you're looking just as sweet as ever."

Hiro moved along the line of plants, talking in a relaxed manner and calling them by name. He stopped in front of a rather sorry looking oleander whose leaves were drooping noticeably.

"Lea, beautiful, you're just not looking your best today. You've got to try harder." He turned to S.S. 101. "Have you been shouting at them again?"

S.S. 101 didn't answer.

"I asked you a question, Sergeant," said Hiro.

S.S. 101's eyes shifted round. "You told me to speak to them," he said sulkily.

"I said talk, not shout. Encourage them, don't threaten them. It doesn't do any good."

"It keeps the weeds in order," muttered S.S. 101.

"What did you say?" asked Hiro. A sudden flicker on the control panel saved S.S. 101 from answering Hiro's question.

"We've got a contact," he said.

Hiro joined him at the controls. He stared grimly at the readings. "It's fast," he said. "Very fast. And big. And if I'm not mistaken..."

"It's heading straight for us."

"Exactly."

Inside Terrahawk, Captain Mary Falconer was reading aloud from Shakespeare's 23rd sonnet while Dr 'Tiger' Ninestein had just blasted his 599th flying saucer on his favourite video game. Before he could zap the 600th, Hiro's face filled the Video Display Unit.

"Slight rise in blood pressure," observed TIM, the Doctor's implant monitor. Ninestein ignored him.

"We have a contact," said Hiro.

"Sensors?" asked Ninestein.

"Unmanned and unarmed. Possible meteor. Collision course. E.T.A. 12 seconds."

"Knock it out, Hiro."

"Ten-ten!"

Hiro turned from his communicator.

"You heard him, Sergeant," he barked. "Open fire!"

Along the length of Spacehawk's hull, the zeroids went into action, launching a massive broadside into the heart of the oncoming meteor.

"It's still coming," said S.S. 101. "Impact in 5 seconds."

"Activate the missile launchers," ordered Hiro.

The fiery ball of rock was now close enough to be seen with the naked eye.

"Ten-ten. Three seconds to impact."

The first missiles exploded on target, but still the flaming mass hurtled closer.

"2 seconds... one..."

Suddenly, as the second batch of missiles hit home, there was a blinding flash of light and Spacehawk rocked like a cork in the surf. The whole ship shuddered violently, and Hiro was flung against the controls.

Eventually the stabilisers regained control and Hiro contacted Ninestein.

"We got it," he said. "Complete disintegration."

Ninestein looked up from his instruments on board Terrahawk.

"Ten-zero, Hiro."

"What do you mean?" asked Hiro, startled. "We've just blasted it out of

the sky. I saw it with my own eyes!"

"Expect the unexpected," said Ninestein. "Our readings show a second object was travelling in the meteor's wake—if it *was* a meteor. It changed course in the last seconds and now it's through."

"Is it manned?" asked Hiro.

Ninestein nodded back at the VDU. "And armed. We've got a ten-forty here."

Sergeant Major Zero unplugged his sensors from the controls and drew in his cables.

"Better make that a ten-fifty, Doctor," he said. "Whatever that thing is, it's making a direct course for the UN High Command Headquarters!"

"Since when did you start giving—"

"Blood pressure, Doctor—" interrupted TIM.

"Knock it off!" snarled Ninestein. "Kate—you've got a ten-fifty!"

Inside the egg-like cockpit of Hawkwing, Kate acknowledged Ninestein's order in the customary Terrahawks manner. "Ten-ten!" she said briskly. "Hawkeye—are you on the wing?"

Lieutenant Hawkeye's easy, familiar drawl answered back from the gun bay on the top of Hawkwing's wing. "Ten-ten, ma'am—let's hit it!"

Kate activated Hawkwing's powerful Camberling SGV 9 Turbo Thrust and the safety clamps on Hawkwing swung aside as the sleek craft accelerated into the launch tunnel. The tunnel doors opened and Hawkwing sped through the swirling vortex of water, burst up through the surface of the pool and raced skywards.

While Hawkwing's on-board computers locked into the alien intruder's flight path, Kate radioed back to Ninestein for more information.

"I don't know..." said Ninestein with a frown. "These readings seem confused. Sometimes they indicate several beings on board, and sometimes just one..."

"What does that mean?" asked Kate.

"I don't know... but I'm working on a theory."

Hawkeye cut into the conversation.

"Target should be in range in two minutes," he said.

"Ten-ten, Hawkeye—take it away."

"Just make sure you keep this thing steady."

When they came in range of the alien craft, Hawkeye opened up with the High Energy Laser Cannons.

"Right on the button!" said Kate, but then a puzzled look crossed her features as she studied the scope. "Give them another blast, Hawkeye."

"Ten-ten, ma'am."

Hawkeye fired the lasers again and as Kate studied the scope her sense of unease deepened. It seemed impossible, but—the blasts from the laser cannons were passing directly through the target, leaving it completely unharmed!

Hawkeye's voice cut across her

thoughts. "Got a visual here, ma'am... Well, I'll be—"

Kate looked up from her controls. Although she had been trained to expect the unexpected, the sight that greeted her made her eyes widen in surprise. There, speeding along ahead of her, clustered round a giant honeycomb, was what looked like a swarm of monster bees.

"Firing missiles," said Hawkeye.

Kate and Hawkeye watched as the missiles zoomed in on their target. As they homed in, the bees flew off the honeycomb and began spinning round it at great speed. The missiles slammed into the honeycomb and exploded with a deafening roar.

"Good shooting, Hawkeye."

"Thanks ma'am. But it's not over yet."

Hawkeye was right. Debris from the explosion was hitting Hawkwing in several places. It was thick and sticky, and everywhere it landed there was a loud hissing sound as it began to eat its way through Hawkwing's wing.

Ninestein's voice came over the communicator.

"Unless I'm wrong, it's a special kind of acid, Kate," he said. "If it eats through the wing it will explode. You know what to do."

"Ten-ten."

Kate busied herself at the controls as the acid ate its way through the outer casing of the wing. A powerful hydraulic arm reached up from the Egg and moved towards the Gun Bay. Flaps in the wing opened wide and the Gun Bay itself passed through them and moved down to attach itself to the back of the Egg.

"You with me, Hawkeye?"

"Ten-ten."

"Breakaway!"

Kate hit the controls again and the Egg, with the Gun Bay still attached, broke away from the huge wing section. As it dived towards earth, small auxiliary wings swept out from the fuselage, the tail fins angled down, and Kate gained full control. A thunderous explosion above them told them they'd made it just in time.

"Nice work," said Ninestein. "Did the explosion get any of those bees?"

"Ten-zero, Doctor, and what's more—they're coming after us."

Kate looked out of the window where three bees were racing towards them. As they got close they began to somersault, and three white bolts of energy flashed from their stings.

"Steady... steady..." said Hawkeye calmly, as the craft jerked violently under the impact of the bolts. Using his computer-assisted eyesight to offset the wildly rocking ship, he loosed off a long blast on the Laser Cannons. The three bees disintegrated in a ball of fire.

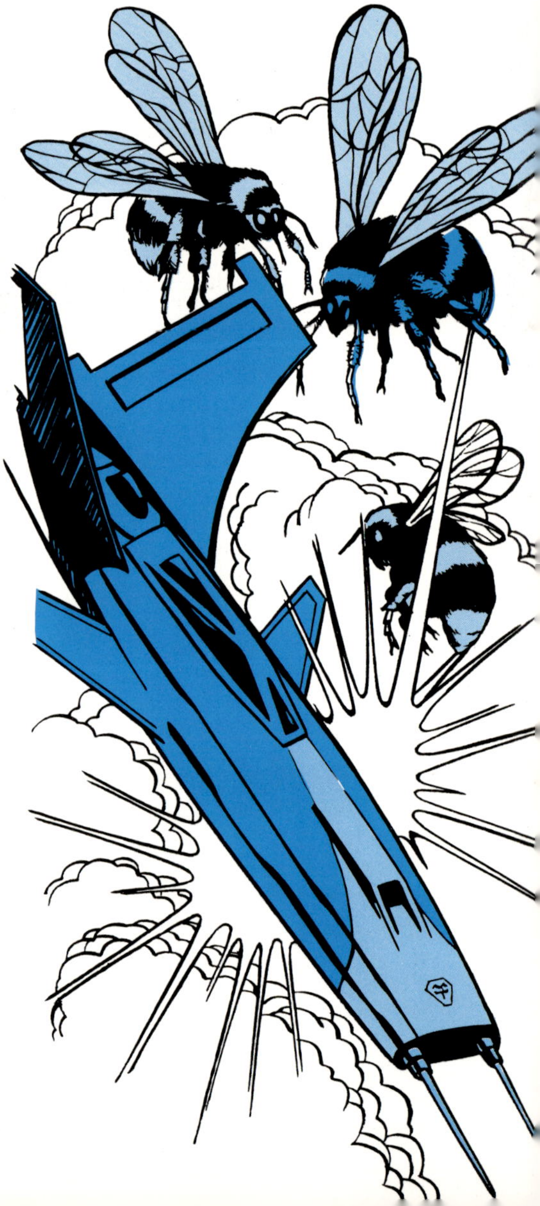

"At least they can be swatted," observed Hawkeye laconically.

"That's good to know," answered Kate. "Because there's more of them coming in. Hundreds of them."

"Take evasive action," ordered Ninestein. "We're coming up!"

"Copy."

As Kate flung Hawkwing through a testing series of manoeuvres in her deadly air battle with the bees, Ninestein, Mary and Sgt. Major Zero prepared to take off in Terrahawk.

"Everyone on board?" asked Ninestein.

"Twenty of my very best men," said Sgt. Major Zero proudly.

"Then let's get on with it."

Sgt. Major Zero bounced onto the instrument panel and two arms extended from their hatches to hold him in position.

"Ready for lift-off."

"Ten-fifty."

"Ten-ten."

The softly glowing panels became brighter, more transparent, as the sound of the thrusters rose from a whine to a roar. Slowly at first, Battlehawk rose vertically inside its launch shaft and began rotating until it stood upright on its tail. Then, with a shattering explosion of sound, Battlehawk's photon drive burst into action and the magnificent craft hurtled upward.

Above the launch tunnel, the ground shook with a sound like distant thunder. The luxurious White House opened, the walls folded away and the roof moved back. Suddenly, like some monster from the deep bursting free, Battlehawk shot from its launch tunnel with a screaming howl of pure power and climbed up into the sky.

Ninestein got Hiro on the VDU. "Can you get me a visual on Hawkwing?" he asked.

"Ten-ten, Doctor—but it doesn't look good."

Hiro's face on the VDU was replaced by an aerial view of an apparently uninhabited section of thick jungle. As the picture zoomed downwards, Ninestein was able to make out a clearing and, in it, smoking from a hole in the fuselage, was what remained of Hawkwing. Around the wreck, in a menacing ring, were hundreds of deadly bees.

"I've fed the co-ordinates into your on-board computer," said Hiro.

Ninestein turned away from the VDU. "Prepare to launch Battletank."

"Ten-ten."

A faint voice came over the communicators. They recognised it immediately as Kate's. "Ten-ninety... we've got a ten-ninety here. Those things have got us surrounded... they're coming closer... this is a ten-ninety... they're getting nearer!"

Ninestein looked up at the VDU.

The ring of bees was closing in on Kate and Hawkeye. "We copy, Kate," he said. "How's Hawkeye?"

"I'm fine..." Hawkeye broke in.

"Good. Hiro—what's our E.T.A.?" Ninestein's mind was working overtime and he was punching buttons on his control panel.

"Seven minutes, twenty three seconds," said Hiro.

"Okay—now listen good, Kate. Have you got that infernal music machine with you?"

"Ten-ten."

"Right—here's what I want you to do..."

When Battlehawk landed on the edge of the jungle clearing, Ninestein, Mary and Sgt. Major Zero were relieved to see that Ninestein's plan had worked. Instead of finding the bees swarming over the crippled Hawkwing, they saw them wandering about the jungle floor in disarray, bumping into each other. As the sounds of the photon drive faded away, they became aware of a strange, high pitched sound coming from Hawkwing.

"Get Battletank on the ground," ordered Ninestein.

"Ten-ten!" replied Sgt. Major Zero.

Ninestein and Mary disembarked from Battlehawk and made their way towards a particularly large, brightly coloured bee that was shambling around some distance away from the others. As they got close to it the high-pitched sound from Hawkwing suddenly stopped.

Immediately, the bee stiffened, and reared up on its hind legs. With an angry buzz of triumph it leapt onto Ninestein, knocking him to the ground. Ninestein was almost smothered as the bee's head bore down on him. Looking into the huge black eyes, Ninestein imagined he saw, deep within them, the snarling, spitting, vengeful face of Zelda, evil Imperial Queen of the Planet Guk. A weird buzzing voice rang through his brain.

"Die, scum! I am the Queen! Die, despicable human!"

"Can it, bug-eyes!" said Ninestein, struggling to throw the bee off. He couldn't.

Ninestein fought in vain as the bee rose up ready to plunge her massive barbed sting into his unprotected stomach.

And then there was a sudden flash of light and the bee rolled to one side, mortally wounded. As it writhed in its death-throes it began to fade, and then suddenly it vanished, as did all the other bees along with it. Zelda was reclaiming her own.

Ninestein looked round to see Sgt. Major Zero standing by Battletank. He gave him a casual salute and the Sgt. Major's eyes lit up.

"Sorry about this packing up," said Kate, approaching from Hawkwing and patting her music machine. "What happened?"

"Nothing much," said Ninestein. "I know some bees communicate by doing a fast, noisy, vibrating dance, so I worked out an oscillating pattern to foul up their systems. And once the queen bee had gone the rest were useless."

Sgt. Major Zero's voice interrupted further explanation.

"Lieutenant Hiro's been trying to reach you for the last five minutes," he said.

Ninestein went back to the VDU. "What is it, Hiro?"

"Nothing, sir. It doesn't matter now."

"Come on, Hiro—spit it out!"

S.S. 101 rolled onto the side of the screen. "Lieutenant Hiro wanted you to save one of those bees for his Venus Fly Trap," said S.S. 101. "But he was afraid of what you'd say if he asked."

"He was right," said Ninestein. "Buzz off!"

A SUDDEN UNPROVOKED ATTACK FROM THE BLACKNESS OF SPACE WAS JUST THE BEGINNING. IT WOULD ALL LEAD UP TO...
NINESTEIN'S BIG DROP!
TEN-TEN, HIRO— KNOCK IT OUT!
LOOKS LIKE WE GOT A TEN-FORTY HERE!
SPACEHAWK'S ZEROIDS GO INTO ACTION...
W-HOOOM!
BUT...
LIEUTENANT, LOOK OUT THERE- FLOATING IN THE DEBRIS...
IT LOOKS LIKE SOME KIND OF... SURVIVAL POD!
POWERFUL RECOVERY CABLES SNAKE OUT...

AND...
DOCTOR–THIS POD SURVIVED THE BLAST!
BRING IT DOWN, HIRO–WE'LL TAKE A LOOK
SO...
ZOW!!
ZOOM!
IT HAS ALL THE CHARACTERISTICS OF A GIANT COCOON!
LIKE A CATERPILLAR BEFORE IT CHANGES TO A BUTTERFLY?
GET BACK! THERE'S SOMETHING MOVING IN THERE!
IT MIGHT BE CHANGING–JUST LIKE BUTTERFLIES DO!
SUDDENLY...
SOME BUTTERFLY!
FLAMING THUNDERBOLTS!

IT'S GOT TIGER! OPEN FIRE SERGEANT!
VERY WELL. READY MEN...AIM...
YUK! IT'S LIKE QUICK-SETTING RUBBER!
I CAN'T MOVE!
GLOOOP!
STICKY SUBSTANCE... MUST ANALYSE...
KATE! WE'RE STUCK! HAWKWING'S GOT A TEN-FIFTY!
TEN-TEN
SENSORS INDICATE IT'S A KIND OF RUBBER...
WITHIN 90 SECONDS...
ZOW!
Z-ZZZITT!!
IT'S USING A PARTICLE ACCELERATOR!
MAKE IT OPEN SEASON ON DRAGONS, HAWKEYE!
BULLSEYE! IT'S DROPPED NINESTEIN!
BDUI!
BDUI!
BDUI!

HAWKEYE LEAPS INTO ACTION...
HAWKWING'S TOO FAST TO EFFECT A PROPER RESCUE!
DON'T WORRY, KATE–I'M GOING AFTER HIM.
AND...
WHOOOOSH!!!
GET AWAY FROM ME! THAT THING WON'T CARRY US BOTH!
GRAB HOLD! IT MIGHT SLOW US DOWN!
ON THE GROUND...
GLOOOSH!
MEN– OPEN FIRE!
LET'S HOPE ZERO ANALYSED THAT STUFF CORRECTLY
IT HELD! WELL DONE, MEN!
MARY EXPLAINS WHAT HAPPENED...
BY THE TIME THE ENERGISED SALT WATER HAD DISINTEGRATED THE DOME, ZERO HAD WORKED OUT A FORMULA FOR IT...
BUT HOW DID YOU KNOW THAT THE WATER WOULD HAVE THAT EFFECT?
WE DIDN'T...
BUT WHEN A DRAGON TAKES A DIVE IN YOUR POOL...
YOU SURE GET A CHANCE TO FIND OUT!
FLAMING THUNDERBOLTS!

HARDWARE SPECIFICATION

HUDSON—NINESTEIN'S ROLLER

HUDSON is a car with a difference in the year 2020—a vintage Rolls Royce from the late 1980s with one or two minor modifications...

HUDSON has intelligence and can speak. His synthesized voice is perfect—not the slightest trace of robotics.

HUDSON is the perfect servant—and a gentleman; a gentleman's gentleman. A combination of advanced technology, high performance, space and comfort.

HUDSON will respond to spoken commands and whilst he can be driven, he is equally happy to drive himself, thus allowing the driver to swing round in his seat to face his passengers at their circular table.

HUDSON is 'trained' to recognise and obey only the voice of his owner. If anyone tries to imitate that voice they won't fool HUDSON. He knows his master... the way he thinks... what makes him tick.

HUDSON is left-hand drive. On the right is a mini-perch for Sergeant Major Zero. This very special Rolls Royce is finished in a very special colour: CHAMELEON.

HUDSON can change colour to suit a mood, to compliment a lady's gown, or camouflage himself in dangerous situations.

HUDSON has electronic 'eyes' on the dashboard and under the front and rear bumpers, so he is able to keep himself very well informed.

HUDSON's 'Silver Lady' retracts to be replaced by a Microzoid which has all the functions of a Zeroid.

For the technically minded: **H** Heuristic
U Universal
D Driver with
S Sensory and
O Orbital
N Navigation

Classified Information

Ninestein Vs. Ninestein

Zelda gazed at the bowl full of purple liquid and her shrill, unearthly laughter pierced the eerie silence of her Mars base. She took a pinch of yellow powder from a glass phial and dropped it into the bowl. The purple liquid bubbled and swirled, and when it came to rest, there, floating under the surface, was a perfect likeness of Tiger Ninestein. Zelda hugged herself with evil glee.

"You have been lucky, Ninestein," she croaked, "very lucky. Your loathsome courage has made you lucky. The idiotic bravery of your numbskull comrades in Terrahawks has managed to save earth so far." Zelda dropped some green powder in the bowl and Ninestein's likeness was swallowed up in green and orange flames. "But the time for luck has passed," Zelda continued, shivering with delight at the prospect of Ninestein's downfall. "Your shabby heroics and footling sense of honour have provided me with the perfect weapon for your destruction... yourself!"

Zelda leant forward and leered into the bowl of liquid. "Do you like my plan, Ninestein? Does it appeal to you?" she slobbered. "To be killed by your own hands should be quite an experience! And the monster I have chosen to start my plan is with me now—come forth, Kuzeba!"

Zelda held up a crooked finger, and from out of the darkness, Kuzeba stepped forward. His appearance was that of a human being and he was dressed in the uniform of a space freighter company.

"Are you ready to serve?" asked Zelda.

"I am, my queen," Kuzeba replied in perfect English.

Zelda drank the purple liquid. "Then be on your way," she ordered, wiping her lips with the back of her hand. "Go now. Yung-Star has already gained access to an earth freighter. Your documents are in order. Go aboard the freighter and carry out my plans!"

"Yes, my queen," said Kuzeba. He nodded, bowed politely, and left.

As the echo of his footsteps faded away there was only the distant dripping of water and the chilling sound of Zelda's own grotesquely confident chuckling.

On Spacehawk, Hiro had a problem.

"Got an unmanned contact, but it's out of range," he explained to Ninestein on the VDU. "Should I investigate with Treehawk?"

"What's it doing?" asked Ninestein.

"Nothing," said Hiro. "It's not even interfering with regular traffic."

"Keep your eye on it," ordered Ninestein.

Sgt. Major Zero, who was plugged into the controls, swivelled round to face him. "There was a message from command," said Zero.

"Urgent?" Ninestein asked, his voice tinged with sarcasm.

"No, sir. They're sending a man down to see you. Professor Knutt. He'll be arriving at the pick-up point this afternoon. Shall I send Hudson to get him?"

"What does he want?" asked Mary.

"They didn't say. He'll tell you when he arrives."

"Send Hudson with one of your men. And tell him to put the shutters up until he's safely back here."

"Ten-ten, sir!" said Zero.

Hiro's face came back on the VDU. He look worried. "That contact," he said. "It's sending out an extremely faint energy beam. I've fed the co-ordinates into the computer. It's somewhere near you, but it's far too weak to offer any threat."

Ninestein rubbed his chin thoughtfully. The beam was directed towards a spot on the route to the pick-up point.

"Sgt. Major—I want you to go with Hudson. Get him to drop you off at these co-ordinates, and if there's anything the slightest bit wrong—report back immediately!"

"Ten-ten, sir!" said Zero, excited at the prospect of a solo mission, no matter how trivial. He bounced down from his perch and rolled through the zeroidoor.

"You look worried, Tiger," said Mary, when Zero had gone.

"I am," said Ninestein, feeding a long series of numbers into the computer. "It sounds crazy, I know, but I've got this feeling..."

From the way he pronounced the last word, Mary knew it was a feeling she didn't want to share.

Professor Knutt arrived with Zero and Hudson in mid afternoon. Zero said he had discovered nothing suspicious at the co-ordinates Ninestein had given him. As they stood in the special visiting room, away from the vital secrets of Hawknest, Mary did her utmost to lighten Ninestein's mood.

"Ah, Professor Knutt," she smiled, shaking the Professor by the hand, "you're not married, are you?"

"No, why?" answered the Professor.

"I knew a Mr Knutt once. Mr P Knutt. His wife was called Hazel."

Only the Professor laughed at Mary's attempt at a joke. He had every reason to laugh. Why should he care about the name Knutt? After all, it wasn't his real name. It was just another stupid human name. A name without pride. A piffling human sound that had none of the glory and splendour of his own, true name—Kuzeba, loyal servant of Zelda, Imperial Queen of the planet Guk!

Kuzeba placed his large case on the table and opened it. Inside was a strange looking helmet.

"What's that?" asked Ninestein.

"Just a simple recording device," said Kuzeba. "Put it on, please."

"What for?"

"Didn't they tell you? asked Kuzeba, a look of innocent surprise lighting up his face. "It's for the computer."

"What?"

"The computer," Kuzeba e plained. "It's been somewhat... uninspired—indecisive, if you like. We thought we'd give it a new personality. A computer as complex and sensitive as the one at central command needs a strong mind to run it.

This encephalo-tracer will enable us to give your personality to the computer."

"Blood pressure rising..." warned TIM.

"Of course it's rising!" stormed Ninestein. He slapped his fist into the palm of his hand and looked up at the ceiling. "Boffins!" he raged. "We're supposed to be doing a job of work here and you want me to take time out to play nursemaid to a bucket full of nuts and bolts that can't even make up its tiny electronic mind!"

"I'll do it!" piped up a zeroid.

"Be quiet, Number 12," snapped Zero.

"It won't take a minute," said Kuzeba soothingly. "And I do have the correct authorisation. Of course, if you're frightened of a little bit of pain..."

Ninestein grabbed the helmet and put it on his head.

"Let's get it over with," he growled.

Kuzeba arranged some dials on the helmet and Ninestein felt a mild tickling sensation in his head. On top of the helmet, a single antenna vibrated without sound. Ninestein was beginning to calm down when the ear piercing shriek of the electronic alarm shattered the silence and Hiro's face came onto the VDU.

"Large energy build-up in your area," he said. "The readings are contradictory. The computer can't cope."

Ninestein tore the helmet from his head and was making for the door when suddenly it shattered and, bouncing through came the agitated form of Sgt. Major Zero!

"Sorry about the door, sir!" he said. "I was going to warn you!"

"Who is this imposter?" said the other Sgt. Major Zero angrily. "Permission to blast him, sir?"

"Permission denied!" said Mary, looking from one Zero to the other. They were exactly alike in appearance. There was no physical means of telling them apart and time was running short.

"Zero, quickly—" said Mary to the first Sgt. Major. "Which is better—chalk or cheese?"

Ninestein gaped at her as though she'd lost her mind.

"Better is not a relevant word in this context," said the first Zero. "Chalk is a more accomplished writing instrument while cheese contains the greater protein."

"Zero?" asked Mary of the second Sgt. Major.

"I always thought chalk tasted better, ma'am," he said.

Mary smiled. "Go get him, boy!" she yelled. "Only the real Zero would dare say that!"

Like a ravenous spacehound unleashed, Zero bounced forward, landing right on top of his fake rival.

"Try to impersonate a superior officer, would you?" he cried, bouncing up and down. "You're not fit to polish my circuits!"

Zero bounced higher and higher, smashing down on his phony rival, until finally, the Zelda-made clone cracked open and Zero ground the debris into the floor.

"Nice work, Sgt. Major," said Mary.

"Thank you," said Zero politely.

Neither of them noticed that Kuzeba had pulled out an ugly-looking snub-nosed beam gun and was holding it on Ninestein.

"Get over with the others!" he spat.

Ninestein, his arms raised, moved slowly towards Mary, Number 12 and Zero. Hiro's face flickered back on to the VDU behind them and his anxious voice sounded a desperate warning.

"They're through!" he said. "We hit them with everything we've got, but they're through! You need a ten-fifty down there! I may have damaged them but—" Hiro was cut short when Kuzeba lifted his gun and blasted the screen to smithereens.

"Whining child!" snarled Kuzeba with contempt. "You cannot stop Her Imperial Majesty with mewling infants! The final conflict has started, but you won't live to see it, Ninestein. It's time for you to meet your doom." The door slid open and Kuzeba laughed at the figure that stood there. "Dr Ninestein... this is your death!"

Mary and Ninestein stared in astonishment at the figure in the doorway. The face, the hair, the eyes, the clothes—everything about the figure was frighteningly familiar. And when it spoke, the figure's voice proved beyond doubt that it was indeed a perfect replica of Dr Tiger Ninestein!

"A good likeness, don't you think, Doctor?" the figure asked, entering the room. In the bright light the likeness was even more uncanny. "Zelda's work. She had my body and Zero's down here already. All it needed was your brain patterns, and you very kindly allowed Kuzeba here to steal them from you and transmit them to me."

Zero rolled forward an inch. "And you stole my circuit design electronically when I went to investigate that energy beam!"

"Get back in line, baldy!" the figure barked. "That was a mistake. We didn't realise you had so much ego, such a pathetic obsessive drive to become human!"

"You talk pretty good, but you don't look much to me!" said Ninestein.

His doppelganger smiled. "You don't realise, do you, Doctor?" he said, stepping closer to Ninestein. "That helmet stole every single facet of your personality. I think like you... I act like you... I talk like you... I AM you! Anything you can do—I can do better! I can do everything you are capable of without even extending myself. I walk like you, I smile like you, I eat like—"

"Chew on this, creep!" Ninestein let go with a tremendous left hook to his opponent's chin. He followed up with two straight rights to the nose. "And smile when you're doing it, bigshot!" As he tried another left, his double moved quickly to block it.

"You had the element of surprise there," said the double, "but as this fight wears on, I think you'll find that in boxing ability I am every bit your equal!"

The double rapped Ninestein with three rapid-fire, clubbing blows to the side of the head that sent him

crashing into a chair.

Ninestein picked up the chair and smashed it over his double's head.

"You talk too much!" said Ninestein, felling his stunned double with a rabbit punch.

Zero used the opportunity to blast Kuzeba. Zelda's loyal servant shrieked as he was hit, and then, amid a stream of gruesome curses, he vanished in a puff of smoke.

Ninestein, Mary, Zero and Number 12 raced back to Terrahawk to find that Kate and Hawkeye had already launched Hawkwing and were in the middle of a hair-raising duel with two craft from Zelda's fleet.

"How's it going, Katie?" asked Ninestein.

"Not good," replied Kate calmly. "They've got the beating of us for speed, but I think Hiro may have damaged one of them, because we're leaving it for dead for manoeuvrability."

"Can you take them out?"

"I don't know," said Kate, putting Hawkwing into a steep dive to evade the attack of the saucers. "As soon as we go after one of them, the other one jumps on our tail!"

"I've got a plan," said Ninestein. "Can you take them out over the ocean?"

"I can try..."

"Good. Here's what I want you to do..."

As Kate flung Hawkwing back and forwards across the sky and Hawkeye loosed off venomous bursts of laser cannon fire whenever a target appeared, Ninestein relayed his plan to them. By the time they reached the open sea, Kate was ready to put it to the test.

Using all her skill, Kate dummied the two saucers and set off on a screaming dive towards the sea. The two saucers were quickly on her tail, the beam gun turrets on their silvery domes swivelling to catch Hawkwing in their lines of fire. As the sea rushed up to meet her, Kate warned Hawkeye to hold on tight.

At the last moment, Kate pulled Hawkwing out of the dive and started a shuddering, bone-jarring loop.

One saucer stayed with Hawkwing all the way, but the other, damaged by the zeroids on Spacehawk, clearly did not have the capacity for such a manoeuvre. As Hawkwing swept upwards the second stricken saucer slowed violently and came to a sudden halt, hovering inches above the water.

By this time, Kate, having completed the loop with Hawkwing, was bearing down on the hovering saucer, while the other saucer, hot on Hawkwing's tail, tried to blast her out of the sky. As they zoomed above the waves, the glare of the sun on the sea almost blinded them. The image of the damaged saucer was nearly impossible to make out with the naked eye. But, as the undamaged saucer closed in for the kill, Kate gave the controls the lightest of touches. Hawkwing hopped over the hovering saucer and the undamaged saucer following close behind Kate smashed into its sister ship and exploded, sending a shower of red hot metal hissing into the sea.

"Good work, Kate," said Ninestein in Terrahawk. "This calls for a celebration."

"Champagne and sandwiches?" asked Kate.

Ninestein nodded. "Salmon, egg, salad, tomato, cheese..." Ninestein cast a glance in Zero's direction. The Sgt. Major pretended not to notice. "And a couple with chalk."

"You got it, Tiger!"

HARDWARE SPECIFICATION

THE TERRAHAWK

Function:	command control craft integrated flightdeck of the 'Battlehawk' transporter
Data File Access Code:	HPY:5449:B:88710/TH
Colour:	metallic silver, black and orange
Distinguishing marks:	T-Hawk emblem
Zonal capacity:	Earth atmosphere
Fuel:	hydroctane
Main drive:	twin Jupiter thrust jets
Maximum velocity:	mach point 8 at sea level
Minimum launch time:	22 sec
Fire power:	machine cannon missile launcher one-zero
Armour:	one-zero
Unladen weight:	not specified
Maximum payload:	not specified
Crew (2):	Dr 'Tiger' Ninestein Captain Mary Falconer

The TERRAHAWK is the operational nucleus—the nerve centre of Dr Ninestein's fighting force. As a mobile command centre it can quickly seek out the best vantage point from which to direct operations. In its 'nest' it is the flightdeck of the giant BATTLEHAWK, ready to transport reinforcements and heavy equipment to the battle zone.

It is here at his computer console that Dr Ninestein directs operations and—in his spare time—plays his favourite video game.

Classified Information

THE GOLDEN SKELETON INVASION
A SHIP FROM ZELDA'S FLEET HAS SLIPPED PAST SPACEHAWK ON THE BLIND SIDE OF A FREIGHTER. NOW HAWKWING JOINS THE FRAY.
LOCKED IN, HAWKEYE!
TEN-TEN FIRE!
BUD!!
BUD!!
KREEEEEE!
THAT'S ONE MORE FOR THE GOOD GUYS!
NICE WORK, HAWKEYE! I'M FOLLOWING IT DOWN.
STRIKE ONE NINESTEIN! SHALL WE RETURN TO BASE?
KRAK-A-BOOM!
TEN-ZERO, KATE. STAY WITH THE WRECK TILL WE GET THERE!
AND SO...
ROOAAAR!
WHEN NINESTEIN REACHES THE WRECK...
TAKE HER DOWN, ZERO.
TEN-TEN SIR!
BE CAREFUL! OUR READINGS SUGGEST THERE'S SOMETHING STILL ALIVE DOWN THERE.

NINESTEIN AND MARY INVESTIGATE...
WHAT A MESS! NOTHING COULD SURVIVE THIS!
DON'T BE TOO SURE, MARY–LOOK AT THESE TRACKS!
BUT WHO...OR WHAT COULD HAVE MADE THEM?
THAT'S WHAT WE'RE GOING TO FIND OUT. STAY WITH BATTLE-HAWK, ZERO.
TEN-TEN IF YOU INSIST.
THE TRACKS LEAD TO A CAVE...
LOOKS LIKE THEY'VE GONE TO GROUND. WAIT HERE!
STOW IT, TIGER–I'M WITH YOU ALL THE WAY!
EVENTUALLY...
STEPS!
THEY MUST HAVE BEEN HERE FOR THOUSANDS OF YEARS!
AND...
BRRRR! LOOKS LIKE SOME ANCIENT BURIAL CHAMBER.
I'VE GOT NEWS FOR YOU, TIGER...

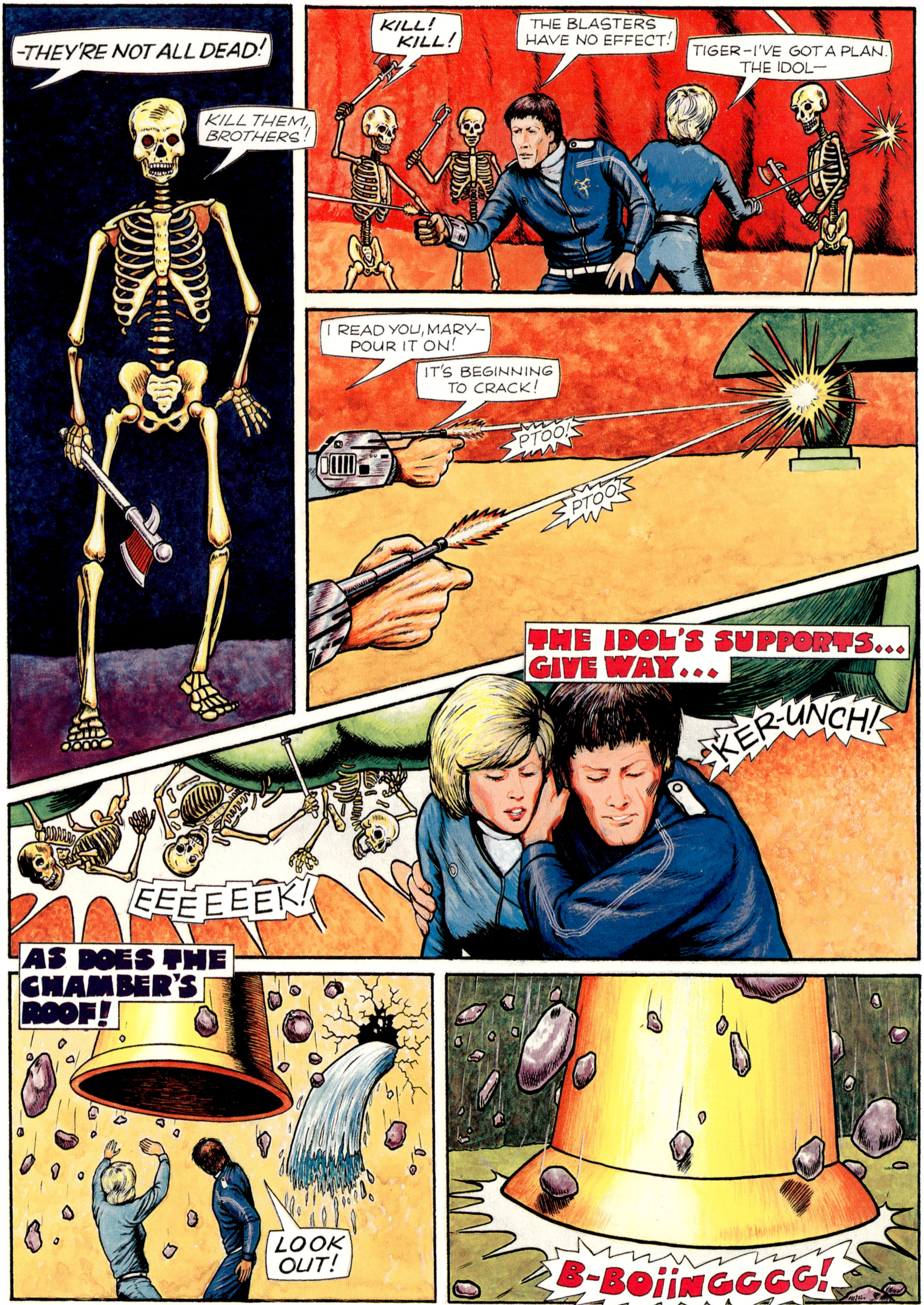
-THEY'RE NOT ALL DEAD!
KILL THEM, BROTHERS!
KILL! KILL!
THE BLASTERS HAVE NO EFFECT!
TIGER–I'VE GOT A PLAN. THE IDOL—
I READ YOU, MARY– POUR IT ON!
IT'S BEGINNING TO CRACK!
PTOO!
PTOO!
THE IDOL'S SUPPORTS... GIVE WAY...
KER-UNCH!
EEEEEEK!
AS DOES THE CHAMBER'S ROOF!
LOOK OUT!
B-BOIINGGGG!

MEANWHILE, SGT. MAJOR ZERO IS GETTING RESTLESS...
THAT WAS CLOSE!
IT'S GOING TO GET CLOSER. THE WATER'S UP TO MY KNEES AND STILL RISING!
THEY'RE IN TROUBLE! I CAN FEEL IT! BUT I'VE GOT MY ORDERS
BLOW THE ORDERS! ST... ROLL...
...ON!
AND...
KER-LANGGG!
YOU WERE WONDERFUL, SGT. MAJOR!
YOU DISOBEYED AN ORDER. HAVEN'T I WARNED YOU ABOUT THAT BEFORE?
IT DOESN'T SEEM TO RING A BELL, SIR.

HARDWARE SPECIFICATION

THE BATTLEHAWK

Function:	heavy transporter and mass deployment unit
Data File Access Code:	3387:ZKKT:2:92739/TH
Colour:	metallic silver, black and orange
Distinguishing marks:	T-Hawk emblem
Zonal capacity:	Earth atmosphere
Fuel:	hydroctane
Main drive:	McKinley-Thor photonic thrust drive
Maximum velocity:	mach 5 at 78,000′
Minimum launch time:	186 secs
Fire power:	marauder machine cannon megazoid battletank one-zero
Armour:	one-zero
Unladen weight:	not specified
Maximum payload:	not specified
Crew:	Zeroids

Controlled from the flightdeck within the TERRAHAWK, the BATTLEHAWK is the flagship of the fleet. It is a giant transport craft and can 'drop' and recover a Battletank in flight, and carries its own awesome fire power. The TERRAHAWK can operate as an integral part of the Battlehawk or on its own.

From a horizontal position at the base of its launch tower, the Battlehawk begins to lift its nose until it is standing vertically. The fire doors open as the photon drive explodes into action and the Battlehawk slowly climbs at increasing speed. The 'White House' front swings forward and the roof opens as the Battlehawk bursts out of the launch shaft to climb skywards.

Classified Information

PERSONNEL PROFILE

SPACE SERGEANT 101

RESTRICTED

©Anderson Burr Pictures Ltd.

subject: Space Sergeant 101

rank: sergeant
genetic type: Zeroid (type AC)
date of origin: November 2018
(batch 874/TH)
place of origin: made in Japan
security rating: ZZ, subject to test
colour:
weight: 100 tons maximum
data bank: 160 K
power source: Iranium
re-order number: 8852901

service reports:

No malfunctions reported. 101 is a specially-modified type AC version, programmed to exercise supervisory and organisational tasks when remote from human direction.

military evaluation:

Insufficient data.

special characteristics:

Space Sergeant 101 shows signs of developing 'emotional' characteristics thought to be connected with unidentified properties of the power source. No harmful effects.

PERSONNEL PROFILE

ZERO

RESTRICTED

subject: Zero

rank: sergeant major
genetic type: zeroid (type AA)
date of origin: October 2018 (batch 873/TH)
place of origin: made in Japan
security rating: ZZ subject to test
colour:
weight: 100 tons
data bank: 180K
power source: Iranium
re-order number: 8851996

service reports:

The sole surviving example of prototype Zeroid. No reported functional weaknesses. Observations indicate that logic circuits are subject to external manipulation under varying degrees of environmental stress. All three previous batch stereotypes were destroyed on a Search and Rescue mission, the success of which was due to their unaccountable and unprogrammed 'heroics'. A very sophisticated design.

military evaluation:

Insufficient data.

special characteristics:

The power nucleus of this Zeroid is a unique Iranium crystal from the planet Jupiter. Hiro, who designed and built the prototypes, believes that this power source had induced 'emotions' normally associated only with humanoid life forms, and Sergeant Major Zero constantly confirms his agreement with this diagnosis. He desperately wants to be human, and likes to make 'decisions' which infuriates Doctor Ninestein, and tends to provoke sympathy from Mary.

HARDWARE SPECIFICATION

THE HAWKWING

Function:	atmospheric interceptor
Data File Access Code:	8761:JABW:3:52853/TH
Colour:	metallic silver, black and orange
Distinguishing marks:	T-Hawk emblem
Zonal capacity:	Earth atmosphere/threshold of space
Fuel:	hydroctane
Main drive:	Camberling SGV 9 turbo thrust
Maximum speed:	mach 7.5 at 100,000′
Minimum launch time:	85 seconds
Fire power:	fireflash particle accelerators high energy laser cannon stingwing missile capability
Armour:	one-zero
Unladen weight:	not specified
Maximum payload:	not specified
Crew (2):	egg shell—Kate Kestrel gun bay—Hawkeye

The HAWKWING is launched in an underground tunnel attached to a powerful overhead catapult which accelerates the craft from 0-750 ft per sec in 10 seconds. The catapult releases the Hawkwing, which flies under computer control in the tunnel, curving upwards. In the lake near the base the giant turbine is gathering speed to create a vortex in the water. The timing is critical. The tunnel entrance under the lake opens and the Hawkwing screams through the vortex and climbs skyward as the turbine shuts down and the waters close over to conceal their secret once more.

The Hawkwing is a deadly fighter aircraft which if all else fails can recover its Gunnery Officer from the gun bay and fly directly to its target, sending the entire wing, with its fuel store and explosives, smashing into the enemy position. The crew, safe in the 'egg', fly away at the last second.

The air was bright, crisp and clean, and only the buzzing of insects and the loud, whooping calls of tropical birds broke the silence as Hiro made his way back to Hawknest with some fresh samples of jungle vegetation. The hour he had spent in the rain forests had been a particularly fruitful one, and he was anxious to get back and study his new specimens. As he gazed at the splendid white colonial style mansion house gleaming in the early morning sun, Hiro found it hard to imagine that at that very moment the actual existence of the world itself was still under threat from the vile ambitions of that cruel and vicious paranoid maniac Zelda, the demented android who was Imperial Queen of the planet Guk.

Hiro passed the magnificent bowl-shaped sunken rose garden with its spectacular sculpture, and stopped in front of what looked like an ancient tree. He raised a clenched fist to the tree and the electronic signature in his ring activated a door in the tree's trunk. The door opened and Hiro stepped into the elevator inside. The elevator sped down, paused briefly at the bottom of the shaft, then raced horizontally to Hawknest control on Terrahawk.

Hiro stepped out of the lift and walked over to the console, where Ninestein was approaching a score of 700 on his favourite video game.

"I've got some wonderful samples," said Hiro.

"Oh, yeah?" Ninestein's score edged forward.

"Yes. Some of them I haven't seen before."

"Uh-huh." The score passed 700. Just another 56 and he'd break his own record!

"I'm going to have to try and identify them from computer records."

"You do that thing." 746... 747... 748...

"Take this one, for instance," said Hiro, holding up a cactus-like plant in front of Ninestein's face. "It's completely new to me."

Ninestein, his vision impaired by the plant, didn't see the tiny flying saucer that sneaked past his defences on the VDU and knocked out his gun position, putting him out of the game with a score of 749.

"Steady..." cautioned TIM.

"Flaming thunderbolts!" Ninestein complained to Hiro. "Don't you know when to leave a man alone?"

"I just thought you'd like to see this

plant," said Hiro. "It appears to be a rather remarkable specimen." As if to prove it, one of the barbed spikes on the cactus flew off and embedded itself in the end of Ninestein's nose.

"The dart contains certain unusual chemicals..." said TIM. "Prepare for analysis."

Ninestein pulled the tiny dart from his nose and threw it to the ground.

"I've had just about enough!" he said menacingly to Hiro. "You spend half your time talking to a lot of overgrown cabbages, and then when you've got something brand new to talk to—you decide to talk to me. I was on 749!"

Mary came over to try and calm Ninestein down.

"Take it easy, Tiger," she said, dabbing the end of Ninestein's nose with a handkerchief.

"You'd better sit down," advised TIM. "That dart contained a very powerful, unpredictable sedative."

"Uhh...?" asked Ninestein. Already the drug from the plant was beginning to take effect.

Mary led him to a chair as the VDU screen blipped into action and Space Sergeant 101 appeared.

"We've got a ten-thirty," said S.S. 101.

"Ish it zat time already?" slurred Ninestein, his eyelids drooping shut.

Mary immediately took control. "What is it?"

"Sensors indicate a single ship in transit towards earth. No known ship is scheduled for the route it's taking."

"Stay with it, 101!" said Hiro. "I'm on my way!"

"Ten-ten, sir."

"Sorry about the Doctor," said Hiro, nodding towards Ninestein as he made his way to the door. "If you feed TIM's analysis into the computer it should be able to come up with an antidote."

"Sure," said Mary. "Now get up there and do your stuff!"

Hiro made his way to Treehawk and called up Mary on the communicator.

"Ready to go."

"Treehawk—you have a ten-fifty!"

"Hawknest—ten-ten!"

Hiro hit the controls and the sound of heavy machinery rumbled round Hawknest as the man-made tree that housed Treehawk opened like an inverted umbrella. The powerful lift-off drives growled into life and the noise grew louder and louder, rising to an earth-shaking crescendo as the Aliphon Chemical Boosters flared in-

to action, wrenching Treehawk free from the pull of gravity and hurling the silver, black and orange spacecraft up towards space.

When Treehawk docked with Spacehawk, Hiro barely had time to store his plants before S.S. 101 was asking for a ten-forty.

Hiro called back to Hawknest. "We've got a ten-forty," he explained to Mary. "How's Ninestein?"

"Still a bit groggy. That cactus of yours packs a pretty big punch. What's happening up there?"

Hiro checked it out with S.S. 101.

"One craft approaching. Unidentified. Still out of range. Two life forms aboard, also unidentified. No conventional weapons detected, but evidence of an unnaturally large power source."

"Zelda?"

"It could be. I'll give them a warning shot when they get within range."

"I'm sending out Hawkwing."

"Good. No—wait!"

"What is it, Hiro?"

"It's slowing down... it's slowing down at the very edge of our range."

"It's stopped," S.S. 101 chipped in. "And it would appear that it has activated some kind of energy-release system."

"Directed at Spacehawk?" asked Hiro.

S.S. 101 crossed his eyes. "Exactly."

Without warning, a spectral, ice-blue light filled the control room, and Hiro's plants all started moving in their pots, shaking their leaves vigorously as if they were in pain. S.S. 101 tracked a blip on the screen that had started moving towards them.

"I think they're coming in," said S.S. 101.

Hiro didn't answer. As soon as the ice-blue light had appeared, he had slumped forward, his eyes wide open, his tongue lolling from his sagging mouth. S.S. 101 tried to snap him out of whatever evil force had gripped him but Hiro couldn't move. S.S. 101 went back to the controls. The blip had vanished.

Outside Spacehawk, in a ship now so molecularly condensed that it failed to register on any scanners, Zelda, similarly shrunk, was explaining to Yung-Star her plan for the advancement of her infernal empire.

"With Spacehawk out of the way Earth will be wide open to attack," she croaked. "We shall be able to launch attack after attack, an endless stream of loyal servants who will fight for me against the hated Terrahawks!"

"How are we going to destroy Spacehawk?" asked Yung-Star.

"Like this!" grinned Zelda, pulling a small lever. Her craft began vibrating at a phenomenal speed.

"What's happening?" asked Yung-Star. The lights on the ship grew dim and an uneasy, tortured sound of wrenching and tearing grew louder. It formed a fitting backdrop to Zelda's demonic laughter.

"By reducing the ship to a sub-atomic size and activating the hyper-vibratory molecule control systems we are able to pass between the atoms that make up Spacehawk's hull," she explained through the din.

"We're through!" cried Yung-Star with ghoulish anticipation as the sub-microscopic spaceship burst into the seemingly massive flight deck of Spacehawk.

Zelda landed on a speck of soil on the floor. To the naked eye, the speck could not be seen.

To Zelda and Yung-Star, the speck was as huge as the Rocky Mountains.

They climbled out of their ship and immediately reverted to their normal size.

At the controls S.S. 101 was talking to Mary on the VDU.

"I can't waken Hiro, and these readings won't compute," said S.S. 101. A sudden cackle from behind him made him spin round. Before he could open fire, Yung-Star triggered a belt beam. There was a flash and S.S. 101, turned instantly into a super powerful magnet was locked rigid to his perch.

"Now for our friend here," said Zelda, standing over Hiro and bending a small transparent disc into different patterns. Three circular, wreath-like force fields floated down towards Hiro, who immediately snapped awake. He reached for his Terrahawk gun, but his holster was empty.

"Too late," smiled Yung-Star, holding the weapon up between finger and thumb.

"It's never too late!" yelled Hiro defiantly, struggling to his feet.

A blast from Yung-Star's belt-beam sent him crashing back to the floor.

"Don't worry," gloated Zelda. "We won't kill you. We want you to enjoy your experience. You see, you're going on a journey... a journey into the unknown! Do we seem to be getting bigger? I think we do, but that's not the case. You are shrinking, human. My ray will shrink you to a size your puny brain could not comprehend! You are going on a journey through the sub-atomic microverse until you finally cease to exist!"

Hiro looked down at his body. It was true! He was shrinking—his hands, his legs, his feet—even his clothes were getting smaller. And unless he could get hold of Zelda's disc, there was nothing he could do to stop it!

Dredging up every last reserve of his fast-reducing strength, Hiro lunged at Zelda. The evil Imperial Queen side-stepped deftly and Hiro fell heavily against the wall of Spacehawk, crashing into the plant enclosure. Zelda bent double with laughter as the shrinking Lieutenant was buried in a heap of leaves and soil.

"Forget about him," she said finally. "He is finished." She began studying the bits of the control panel not covered by the magnetised zeroids. "Some of these weapons could easily be turned against the earth." She smiled and placed her hand on Yung-Star's shoulder. "Victory is ours—from now on it is only a matter of time."

Hiro, struggling for air and trying to work out how long it would be before he disappeared altogether, was shocked when his rapid computations were suddenly interrupted by a violent screaming sound that exploded inside his brain. Next to him, now the size of a Redwood tree, was the small cactus he had brought on board. The noise in his head got quieter and quieter and was eventually replaced by a gentle mellifluous voice.

"I'm sorry," said the voice. "This kind of communication is new to me—with species such as yourself. I think either that light that so distressed my comrades, or your somewhat... unusual circumstances have enabled us to make a telepathic breakthrough in communications."

Hiro formed the word HELP in his mind and concentrated fiercely.

"Not so loud, please," said the voice. "I can understand you quite easily. But why should I help you?"

"Please."

"You are a good man, Hiro. I sensed it from the other plants. You have treated them well. But I cannot live in a pot. I must have the air, the sun, the rain. Will you promise to return me to where you found me?"

"I promise."

As Hiro watched, the cactus shook, and six tiny barbed darts arced across the room. Four of them embedded themselves in Zelda's neck and two in Yung-Star's.

"Did something just bite you, Mother?" asked Yung-Star, slapping at his neck. "An insect?"

"Yes," agreed Zelda. "Mere pin-pricks to us, but with any luck they'll look the size of elephants to that doomed Terrahawk by now."

But, as the cactus' drugged prickles began to take their toll, Zelda and Yung-Star became increasingly clumsy in their movements, and after he tripped over the Terrahawk gun lying on the floor, Yung-Star's beam belt control smashed against the corner of the console and S.S. 101 was released from its power.

"Open fire!" yelled S.S. 101, and went on the attack. Zelda and Yung-Star, weary and confused by the strength-sapping power of the telepathic cactus' prickles, fell over each other as they struggled to evade the zeroid's onslaught. Neither of them noticed the small transparent disc as it fell from Zelda's pocket and rolled across the floor.

"Quick, Mother!" said Yung-Star. "Shrink us! We can destroy him later!"

"Thatsh exac—, exac—, —thatsh jusht what I'm doing, son."

Zelda, almost overcome with fatigue, peered blearily at the small white box she held up to her eyes.

Her bony fingers pressed two buttons, and she and Yung-Star disappeared from view, instantly miniaturised once again to the size of their ship.

S.S. 101 rolled over to the still-shrinking figure of Hiro.

"Find Zelda's disc!" yelled Hiro.

To S.S. 101 it sounded like a tinny whisper. "You'll have to speak up, sir," he said, opening a hatch and directing a cable down towards Hiro.

Hiro shouted up the end. "Find Zelda's disc!" he repeated.

S.S. 101 clicked into action, scanning the flight deck until his sensors located the disc. He picked it up, placed Hiro in the middle of the floor and folded it exactly according to the computer's directions for reversal.

Hiro grew steadily until he had regained his full height.

"Thank you, Sergeant—that's all," he said briskly.

S.S. 101 looked from Hiro to Zelda's disc.

"What is it, Sergeant?" asked Hiro.

"Have you ever wanted to be taller, sir?" asked 101. "It would be quite easy to—"

"I said that's all, Sergeant," said Hiro, taking the disc from 101. "Prepare a burial detail."

"What for?" asked S.S. 101.

"The plants, Sergeant. Get them back in their pots."

"Yes, sir!"

"And take special care with that new cactus. See it gets whatever it wants until I take it home."

"Are you feeling well, sir?" asked S.S. 101 suspiciously. "You didn't bang your head when you were shrinking, did you?"

"Just do as I say, Sergeant. I'm going to contact Hawknest. Unless Zelda returned to Mars they could be in for a one-fifty!"

But there was no one-fifty, and there wouldn't be one for several hours at lest, even though Zelda and Yung-Star had not returned to Mars.

Finally overcome by the powerful drug from the cactus' prickles, Zelda and Yung-Star had crashed their ship as they tried to pass through Spacehawk's hull. And now, all Yung-Star had to comfort him until his mother recovered her senses sufficiently to get them both out was the grinding and clashing of the sub-atomic microverse and, beneath it, as steady as the dripping of a tap, his mother's dry, rasping, regular snores.

HARDWARE SPECIFICATION

THE TREEHAWK

Function:	Spacehawk service shuttle
Data File Access Code:	4442:PLTB:7:87938/TH
Colour:	metallic silver, black and orange
Distinguishing marks:	T-Hawk emblem
Zonal capacity:	solar 9
Fuel:	trinitrosol
Main drive:	aliphon chemical boosters and underwing atmospheric ram jets
Maximum velocity:	
Aircraft config:	mach point 9
Rocket config:	3.6 million ft per sec
Minimum launch time:	40 seconds
Fire power:	one-zero
Armour:	one-zero
Unladen weight:	not specified
Maximum payload:	not specified
Crew:	Hiro and/or remote control

The TREEHAWK is the space shuttle craft which travels between Earth base and the Spacehawk and services Hiro and his supply requirements.

The Treehawk is so named because its camouflaged launch pad on Earth is a massive artificial tree which opens like an umbrella. At launch the Treehawk is in its rocket configuration but having docked with the Spacehawk and returned to Earth atmosphere, inverted wings unfold to enable it to fly and land as a conventional aircraft.

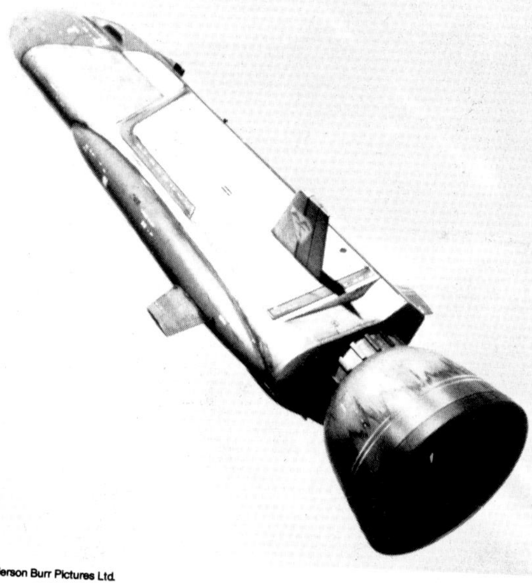

Classified Information

HARDWARE SPECIFICATION

THE SPACEHAWK

Function:	advanced orbital warning and defence station
Data File Access Code:	6199:HJFR:8:33236/TH
Colour:	metallic silver, black and orange
Distinguishing marks:	T-Hawk emblem
Zonal capacity:	solar 9
Fuel:	dilithium crystals
Main drive:	lathirol nuclear pulse drives
Maximum velocity:	2.4 million ft per sec
Minimum launch time:	geo stationary orbit
Fire power:	missile launchers laser cannon one-zero
Armour:	one-zero
Unladen weight:	not specified
Maximum payload:	not specified
Crew:	Hiro 100 Zeroids

The SPACEHAWK is the Terrahawks' first line of defence against Zelda and her forces of destruction. This vast and sophisticated craft is capable of patrolling our solar system and can deliver massive fire power.

The Spacehawk slowly rotates on its lateral axis to provide artificial gravity.

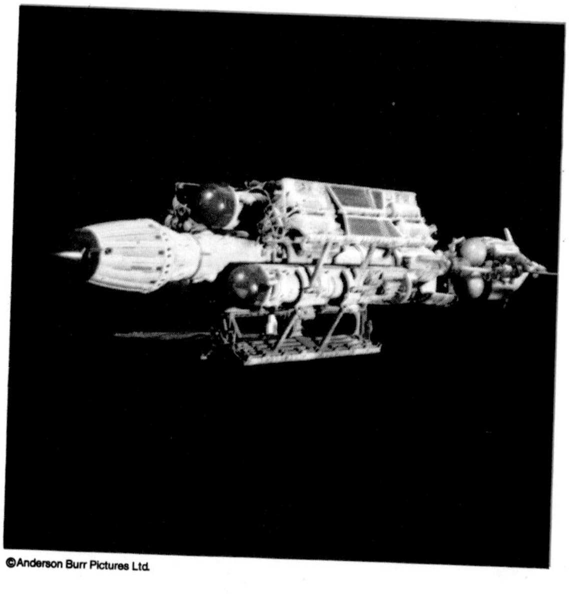

Classified Information

HARDWARE SPECIFICATION

THE BATTLETANK

Function:	airborne ground attack vehicle with robotic controller
Data File Access Code:	9967:YTCP:5:84416/TH
Colour:	metallic silver, black and orange
Distinguishing marks:	T-Hawk emblem
Zonal capacity:	specified ground conditions
Fuel:	hydroctane
Main drive:	barford turbines multi-directional jet thrusters
Maximum velocity:	60 k/h
Maximum launch time:	140 secs
Fire power:	one-zero
Armour:	one-zero
Unladen weight:	not specified
Maximum payload:	not specified
Crew:	Megazoids

The BATTLETANK is a tracked vehicle for conventional ground attack purposes, operated by Megazoid robots, and transported in the cargo hold of the Battlehawk.

The Battletank can be 'dropped' in emergency from the belly of the Battlehawk and uses its multi-directional jet thrusters to set up a powerful downward thrust so as to cushion its ground landing.

The Battletank can equally be 'scooped up' by the low-flying Battlehawk and carried to safe refuge.

Classified Information

TERRAHAWKS CHRONOLOGY

1834 Zelda's official 'birthday'
1973 Professor Stein enters hospital in Texas; Doctor Ninestein's official 'birthday'
1991 Mary Falconer born
1995 Kate Kestrel born
1998 Hawkeye born
2000 Hiro born
2001 Commander John Westley appointed CIC NASA Moon Base
2009 Commander John Westley appointed first officer Mars Landing Mission
2010 Hiro wins honours degrees in maths and physics (age 10)
2011 Kate Kestrel joins NASA Medical Centre; Commander John Westley appointed CIC HQ United Nations Interplanetary Communications (UNIPC)
2012 Mary Falconer's brothers killed
2013 Mary Falconer's father dies; Dr Ninestein retires as CIC United Nations High Command